THIS JOURNAL BELONGS TO

Field Trip Journal - Adventurer Level
By Laena West

July 2017 Copyright © Laena West
All rights reserved.
No part of this book may be reproduced
without prior written consent from the publisher.

San Diego Coastal Explorers Press
ISBN – 13: 978-1973948360
ISBN – 10: 1973948362
First Edition
Printed in the United States of America

Designed, written and compiled by Laena West
Contributing Artists from www.nounproject.com
Alena Artemova - andriwidodo - artworkbear - Blair Adams
Claire Skelly - Ian Porrat - mello - Nerea Martinez Orduna
NOPIXEL - Simon Child - Alex Muraver - Ian Porrat
Vladimar Belochkin

Other titles in this series available on
www.sandiegocoastalexplorers.com

10 9 8 7 6 5 4 3 2 1

TABLE OF CONTENTS

Geography & Me _____ PAGE 6

All About Me _____ PAGE 7

1. _____ PAGE 8

2. _____ PAGE 10

3. _____ PAGE 12

4. _____ PAGE 14

5. _____ PAGE 16

6. _____ PAGE 18

7. _____ PAGE 20

8. _____ PAGE 22

9. _____ PAGE 24

10. _____ PAGE 26

11. _____ PAGE 28

TABLE OF CONTENTS

12. _____ PAGE 30

13. _____ PAGE 32

14. _____ PAGE 34

15. _____ PAGE 36

16. _____ PAGE 38

17. _____ PAGE 40

18. _____ PAGE 42

19. _____ PAGE 44

20. _____ PAGE 46

21. _____ PAGE 48

22. _____ PAGE 50

23. _____ PAGE 52

24. _____ PAGE 54

Table of Contents

Notes & Doodles _____ Page 56

The Year in Review _____ Page 64

Field Trip Checklist _____ Page 66

Field Trip Word Wall _____ Page 67

Navigation - Exploration - Imagination

Can you find where you live?   Where would you like to visit?

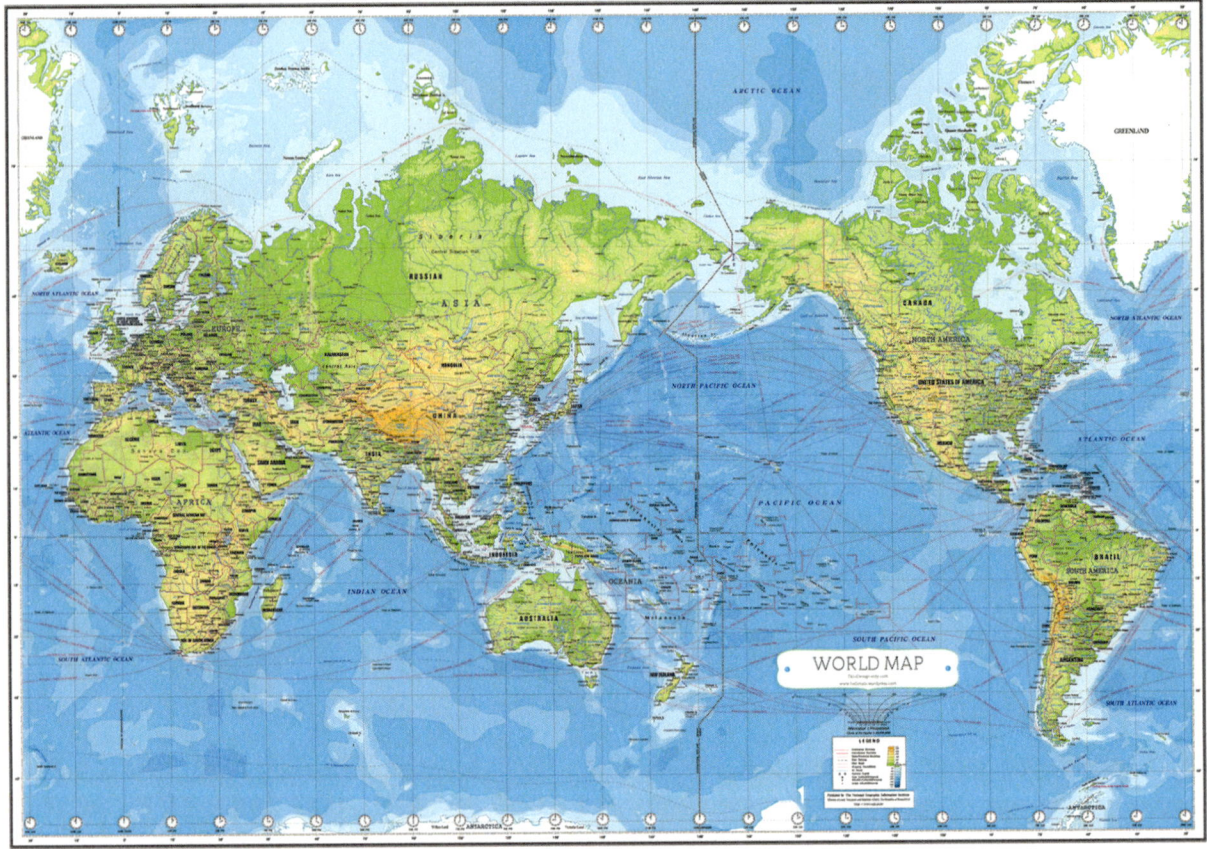

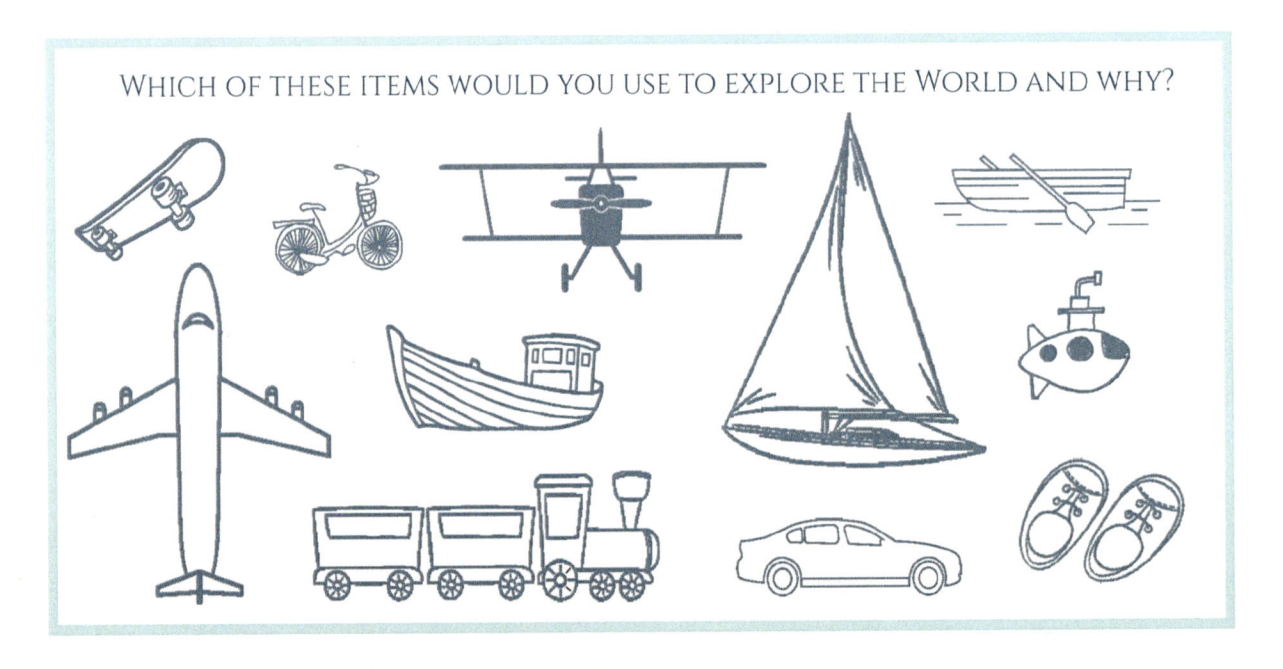

Asia   Africa   North America   South America   Antarctica   Europe

Which of these items would you use to explore the World and why?

All About Me

Draw Create Experience Read Write Learn Explore Imagine Play Discover

~ Nature Notes ~

My Favorite Season

My Favorite Weather

Field Trip Explorer

Name: _____

I am 1 2 3 4 5 6 7 8 9 10 11 Years Old

My Favorite Place to Explore Nature

This is where I live

This is my Family

Country City Suburb Town Farm Boat House Apartment Cabin Skyscraper

Field Trip # 1

Date: _____

Title: _____

Where: _____

How many people from Your family went on the field trip

I can draw My field trip

Today I went to

A Space for Dictation – What did you do on your Field Trip today?

My lunch or snack today

Circle the Weather

Circle the Season

Rate this Trip

☆☆☆☆☆

Would you recommend this trip?   Yes   No

Would you like to Go Back someday?

Yes   Maybe   No

Field Trip # 2

Date: _____

Title: _____

Where: _____

How many people from your family went on the field trip

I can draw my field trip

Today I went to

A Space for Dictation - What did you do on your Field Trip today?

My lunch or snack today

Circle the Weather

Circle the Season

Rate this Trip

☆☆☆☆☆

Would you recommend this trip?   Yes   No

Would you like to Go Back someday?

Yes   Maybe   No

Field Trip # 3

Date: _____

Title: _____

Where: _____

How many people from Your family went on the field trip

I can draw My field trip

Today I went to

A Space for Dictation - What did you do on your Field Trip today?

My lunch or snack today

Circle the Weather

Circle the Season

Rate this Trip

☆ ☆ ☆ ☆ ☆

Would you recommend this trip?   Yes   No

Would you like to Go Back someday?

Yes   Maybe   No

FIELD TRIP # 4　　　　　　　　　**DATE:** _____

TITLE: _____

WHERE: _____

How many people from your family went on the field trip

I can draw my field trip

Today I went to

A Space for Dictation - What did you do on your Field Trip today?

My lunch or snack today

Circle the Weather

Circle the Season

Rate this Trip

☆ ☆ ☆ ☆ ☆

Would you recommend this trip?   Yes   No

Would you like to Go Back someday?

Yes   Maybe   No

FIELD TRIP # 5

DATE: _____

TITLE: _____

WHERE: _____

How many people from your family went on the field trip

I can draw my field trip

Today I went to

A Space for Dictation - What did you do on your Field Trip today?

My lunch or snack today

Circle the Weather

Circle the Season

Rate this Trip
☆☆☆☆☆

Would You recommend this trip?   Yes   No

Would you like to Go Back someday?
Yes   Maybe   No

Field Trip # 6

Date: _____

Title: _____

Where: _____

How many people from your family went on the field trip

I can draw my field trip

Today I went to
_____
_____
_____
_____
_____
_____
_____
_____

A Space for Dictation - What did you do on your Field Trip today?

_____

_____

_____

_____

_____

My lunch or snack today

Circle the Weather

Circle the Season

Rate this Trip

☆☆☆☆☆

Would You recommend this trip? Yes   No

Would you like to Go Back someday?

Yes   Maybe   No

Field Trip # 7

Date: _____

Title: _____

Where: _____

How many people from your family went on the field trip

I can draw my field trip

Today I went to

A Space for Dictation - What did you do on your Field Trip today?

My lunch or snack today

Circle the Weather

Circle the Season

Rate this Trip

☆☆☆☆☆

Would you recommend this trip?   Yes   No

Would you like to Go Back someday?

Yes   Maybe   No

Field Trip # 8

Date: _____

Title: _____

Where: _____

How many people from your family went on the field trip

I can draw my field trip

Today I went to

A Space for Dictation - What did you do on your Field Trip today?

_____
_____
_____
_____
_____

My lunch or snack today

Circle the Weather

Circle the Season

Rate this Trip

☆ ☆ ☆ ☆ ☆

Would You recommend this trip?   Yes   No

Would you like to Go Back someday?

Yes   Maybe   No

Field Trip # 9　　　　　　　　　　　**Date:** _____

Title: _____

Where: _____

How many people from Your family went on the field trip

I can draw My field trip

Today I went to
_____
_____
_____
_____
_____
_____
_____
_____

A Space for Dictation - What did you do on your Field Trip today?

___

My lunch or snack today

Circle the Weather

Circle the Season

Rate this Trip

☆☆☆☆☆

Would You recommend this trip?   Yes   No

Would you like to Go Back someday?

Yes   Maybe   No

Field Trip # 10   **Date:** _____

Title: _____

Where: _____

How many people from your family went on the field trip

I can draw my field trip

Today I went to

A Space for Dictation - What did you do on your Field Trip today?

My lunch or snack today

Circle the Weather

Circle the Season

Rate this Trip

☆☆☆☆☆

Would you recommend this trip?   Yes   No

Would you like to Go Back someday?

Yes   Maybe   No

FIELD TRIP # 11

DATE: _____

TITLE: _____

WHERE: _____

How many people from your family went on the field trip

I can draw my field trip

Today I went to
_____
_____
_____
_____
_____
_____
_____
_____

A Space for Dictation - What did you do on your Field Trip today?

My lunch or snack today

Circle the Weather

Circle the Season

Rate this Trip

☆☆☆☆☆

Would you recommend this trip?   Yes   No

Would you like to Go Back someday?

Yes   Maybe   No

Field Trip # 12

Date: _____

Title: _____

Where: _____

How many people from Your family went on the field trip

I can draw My field trip

Today I went to

A Space for Dictation - What did you do on your Field Trip today?

_____
_____
_____
_____
_____

My lunch or snack today

Circle the Weather

Circle the Season

Rate this Trip

☆ ☆ ☆ ☆ ☆

Would you recommend this trip? Yes   No

Would you like to Go Back someday?

Yes   Maybe   No

31

FIELD TRIP # 13

DATE: _____

TITLE: _____

WHERE: _____

How many people from your family went on the field trip.

I can draw my field trip

Today I went to
_____
_____
_____
_____
_____
_____
_____
_____

A Space for Dictation - What did you do on your Field Trip today?

_____
_____
_____
_____
_____

My lunch or snack today

Circle the Weather

Circle the Season

Rate this Trip

☆ ☆ ☆ ☆ ☆

Would You recommend this trip?   Yes   No

Would you like to Go Back someday?

Yes   Maybe   No

FIELD TRIP # 14　　　　　　　　　　**DATE:** _____

TITLE: _____

WHERE: _____

How many people from your family went on the field trip

I can draw my field trip

Today I went to
_____
_____
_____
_____
_____
_____
_____
_____

A Space for Dictation - What did you do on your Field Trip today?

_____
_____
_____
_____
_____

My lunch or snack today

Circle the Weather

Circle the Season

Rate this Trip

☆ ☆ ☆ ☆ ☆

Would You recommend this trip?   Yes   No

Would you like to Go Back someday?

Yes   Maybe   No

Field Trip # 15   **Date:** _____

Title: _____

Where: _____

How many people from Your family went on the field trip

I can draw my field trip

Today I went to

A Space for Dictation - What did you do on your Field Trip today?

___

My lunch or snack today

Circle the Weather

Circle the Season

Rate this Trip

☆☆☆☆☆

Would You recommend this trip?   Yes   No

Would you like to Go Back someday?

Yes   Maybe   No

Field Trip # 16

Date: _____

Title: _____

Where: _____

How many people from your family went on the field trip

I can draw my field trip

Today I went to

A Space for Dictation - What did you do on your Field Trip today?

My lunch or snack today

Circle the Weather

Circle the Season

Rate this Trip

Would you recommend this trip?   Yes   No

Would you like to go back someday?

Yes   Maybe   No

FIELD TRIP # 17　　　　　　　　　　**DATE:** _____

TITLE: _____

WHERE: _____

How many people from your family went on the field trip

I can draw my field trip

Today I went to

A Space for Dictation – What did you do on your Field Trip today?

My lunch or snack today

Circle the Weather

Circle the Season

Rate this Trip

☆☆☆☆☆

Would You recommend this trip?   Yes   No

Would you like to Go Back someday?

Yes   Maybe   No

Field Trip # 18

Date: _____

Title: _____

Where: _____

How many people from your family went on the field trip

I can draw my field trip

Today I went to
_____
_____
_____
_____
_____
_____
_____
_____
_____

A Space for Dictation - What did you do on your Field Trip today?

My lunch or snack today

Circle the Weather

Circle the Season

Rate this Trip

☆☆☆☆☆

Would you recommend this trip?   Yes   No

Would you like to Go Back someday?

Yes   Maybe   No

FIELD TRIP # 19   DATE:_____

TITLE: _____

WHERE: _____

How many people from your family went on the field trip

I can draw my field trip

Today I went to

A Space for Dictation - What did you do on your Field Trip today?

My lunch or snack today

Circle the Weather

Circle the Season

Rate this Trip

☆☆☆☆☆

Would You recommend this trip?   Yes   No

Would you like to Go Back someday?

Yes   Maybe   No

FIELD TRIP # 20 DATE:_____

TITLE: _____

WHERE: _____

How many people from Your family went on the field trip

I can draw My field trip

Today I went to

A Space for Dictation - What did you do on your Field Trip today?

My lunch or snack today

Circle the Weather

Circle the Season

Rate this Trip

☆☆☆☆☆

Would You recommend this trip?   Yes   No

Would you like to Go Back someday?

Yes   Maybe   No

FIELD TRIP # 21   **DATE:** _____

TITLE: _____

WHERE: _____

How many people from Your family went on the field trip

I can draw my field trip

Today I went to

A Space for Dictation - What did you do on your Field Trip today?

_____
_____
_____
_____
_____

My lunch or snack today

Circle the Weather

Circle the Season

Rate this Trip

☆ ☆ ☆ ☆ ☆

Would You recommend this trip?   Yes   No

Would you like to Go Back someday?

Yes   Maybe   No

FIELD TRIP # 22

DATE: _____

TITLE: _____

WHERE: _____

How many people from your family went on the field trip

I can draw my field trip

Today I went to
_____
_____
_____
_____
_____
_____
_____
_____

A Space for Dictation - What did you do on your Field Trip today?

My lunch or snack today

Circle the Weather

Circle the Season

Rate this Trip

☆ ☆ ☆ ☆ ☆

Would You recommend this trip? Yes   No

Would you like to Go Back someday?

Yes   Maybe   No

Field Trip # 23　　　　　　　　　Date: _____

Title: _____

Where: _____

How many people from Your family went on the field trip

I can draw My field trip

Today I went to

A Space for Dictation - What did you do on your Field Trip today?

My lunch or snack today

Circle the Weather

Circle the Season

Rate this Trip
☆☆☆☆☆

Would You recommend this trip?   Yes   No

Would you like to Go Back someday?
Yes   Maybe   No

53

Field Trip # 24

Date: _____

Title: _____

Where: _____

How many people from your family went on the field trip

I can draw my field trip

Today I went to

A Space for Dictation - What did you do on your Field Trip today?

My lunch or snack today

Circle the Weather

Circle the Season

Rate this Trip

☆ ☆ ☆ ☆ ☆

Would you recommend this trip?   Yes   No

Would you like to go back someday?

Yes   Maybe   No

Notes & Doodles

Notes & Doodles

Notes & Doodles

Notes & Doodles

Notes & Doodles

Notes & Doodles

Notes & Doodles

Notes & Doodles

The Year in Review

My Favorite Trip of the Year:

Favorite animal:

I had the most fun at the...

Funniest Moment on a Field Trip:

Who took you on most of the field trips?

Total # of Trips:

The shoes I wore most often:

REVIEW & REFLECT

I LIKE FIELD TRIPS BECAUSE:
_____
_____
_____

MY FAVORITE PACKED LUNCH TO BRING ON A FIELD TRIP:

FAVORITE MOMENT IN NATURE

PLACES I WOULD LIKE TO VISIT NEXT YEAR:

RATE THIS YEAR OF FIELD TRIPS

☆☆☆☆☆

WOULD YOU RECOMMEND TAKING FIELD TRIPS?

YES   NO

Explorer Checklist

What do you need to make a field trip the best ever?

The Essentials

- [ ] Shoes
- [ ] Hat
- [ ] Jacket
- [ ] Snack
- [ ] Lunch
- [ ] Water-bottle
- [ ] Sunscreen
- [ ] Map
- [ ] Binoculars
- [ ] Watch
- [ ] Sunglasses
- [ ] Compass
- [ ] Pencil
- [ ] Journal
- [ ] _____
- [ ] _____
- [ ] _____

- [ ] Parent's cell phone number #_____ and a plan in case you get separated.

- [ ] Don't forget to say Thank You to the docent for a great field trip!

- [ ] Thank your parents for bringing you to the field trip!

- [ ] Fill out your Field Trip Journal and remember to have fun!

- [ ] _____

Navigation - Exploration - Imagination

Field Trip Word Wall

Where

AIRPORT
AQUARIUM
AUDITORIUM
AVIARY
BAY
BEACH
CITY
COUNTY
DESERT
FACTORY
FARM
FIELD
FOREST
HARBOR
KITCHEN
LABORATORY
LAKE
LIBRARY
MOUNTAIN
MUSEUM
OBSERVATORY
OFFICE
PARK
RANCH
RECYCLING PLANT
REFUGE
RIVER
SCHOOL
STADIUM
STATION
STORE
SYMPHONY
THEATER
WILDERNESS
ZOO

Who

ACTOR
ARCHITECT
ARTIST
ATHLETE
BIOLOGIST
COACH
COOK
DANCER
DENTIST
DOCENT
DOCTOR
DRIVER
ENGINEER
FAMILY
FARMER
FIREFIGHTER
FRIEND
GEOLOGIST
GUIDE
LEADER
LIBRARIAN
MUSICIAN
OFFICER
PERFORMER
PILOT
PROFESSOR
RANGER
RESEARCHER
SAILOR
SCIENTIST
SINGER
TRAINER
VETERINARIAN
WRITER
ZOOKEEPER

When

TODAY
TOMORROW
YESTERDAY

JANUARY
FEBRUARY
MARCH
APRIL
MAY
JUNE
JULY
AUGUST
SEPTEMBER
OCTOBER
NOVEMBER
DECEMBER

SUNDAY
MONDAY
TUESDAY
WEDNESDAY
THURSDAY
FRIDAY
SATURDAY

AUTUMN/FALL
WINTER
SPRING
SUMMER

MORNING
AFTERNOON
EVENING
NIGHT

FOR TIPS ON USING THIS BOOK AND TO
CHECK OUT OUR OTHER FUN BOOKS VISIT US AT
www.sandiegocoastalexplorers.com
HAPPY EXPLORING!